LIVING AN EXTRAORDINARY LIFE

Unlocking the Secrets to Personal Growth, Fulfillment, and Lasting Happiness

IVAN BOSEMAN

Copyright © 2024 by Ivan Boseman

All rights reserved. No part of this publication may be reproduced, distributed, or transmitted in any form or by any means, including photocopying, recording, or other electronic or mechanical methods, without the prior written permission of the publisher, except in the case of brief quotations embodied in critical reviews and certain other non-commercial uses permitted by copyright law.

TABLE OF CONTENTS

Introduction 8
   What Does It Mean to Live an Extraordinary Life? 9
   The Myth of the "Perfect Life" 11
   Why Most People Settle for Mediocrity 13
   The Roadmap to an Extraordinary Life 16

Part 1 21
Mindset Mastery 21
   The Power of Belief 21
   The Science Behind Mindset 23
   How to Rewire Your Thoughts for Success 25
   Overcoming Limiting Beliefs 26
   Identifying Your Self-Imposed Barriers 28
   Strategies to Break Free 29
   Building Resilience 31
   How to Embrace Failure as a Stepping Stone 32

- Developing Emotional and Mental Toughness 33
- The Importance of Self-Awareness ... 34
- Understanding Your Strengths and Weaknesses 35
- Creating a Personal Growth Plan 36

Part 2 38

Purpose and Passion 38
- Discovering Your Purpose 38
- How to Find What Truly Drives You ... 40
- Aligning Your Purpose with Your Actions 41
- The Power of Passion 43
- How Passion Fuels an Extraordinary Life 44
- Overcoming the Fear of Pursuing Your Passion 46
- Living with Intention 47
- How to Make Each Day Meaningful ... 49
- Creating and Sticking to Life Goals ... 50

Part 3 52

Habits of High Achievers 52
- The Daily Routines of Extraordinary People 53

How Morning Routines Can Transform Your Life 54

The Power of Consistency 56

Mastering Time and Focus 57

Prioritizing What Truly Matters 59

Avoiding Distractions and Procrastination 60

Health and Wellness for Optimal Living 61

Why Physical Health is Non-Negotiable 63

Mental and Emotional Wellness Practices 65

Part 4 67

Building Meaningful Relationships 67

The Power of Positive Relationships .. 67

How Your Circle Influences Your Life . 69

Building Supportive, Encouraging Connections 71

The Art of Effective Communication .. 72

How to Be a Better Listener 74

Speaking with Purpose and Clarity ... 75

Developing Empathy and Compassion 76

How Empathy Leads to Better Relationships 78

The Ripple Effect of Kindness 79

Part 5 82

Overcoming Challenges 82

Facing Adversity with Courage 82

Why Hard Times Are Crucial for Growth 84

Strategies to Handle Life's Setbacks . 85

Developing a Problem-Solving Mindset 87

How to Navigate Difficult Decisions .. 88

Staying Calm Under Pressure 90

Managing Stress and Burnout 91

Techniques to Protect Your Mental Health 93

Recognizing the Signs and Taking Action 94

Part 6 97

Financial Freedom and Independence .. 97

The Mindset of Wealth 97

How Financial Success Relates to an Extraordinary Life 99

Shifting to an Abundance Mentality 100

Building Long-Term Wealth 102

Strategies for Saving, Investing, and Growing Your Finances 104

Escaping the Rat Race 106

How to Design a Life of Freedom and Flexibility 108

Part 7 111

Leaving a Lasting Legacy 111

The Importance of Giving Back 111

How Contribution Leads to Fulfillment 113

Finding Causes that Align with Your Values 114

Creating a Life of Impact 116

How to Inspire and Lead Others 117

Living a Legacy That Outlives You .. 119

Conclusion 123

Embracing the Journey, Not Just the Destination 123

Celebrating Your Progress, No Matter How Small 126

Final Words on Living an Extraordinary Life 129

INTRODUCTION

Living an extraordinary life means different things to different people. For some, it's about achieving financial success or career milestones, while for others, it's about deep personal fulfillment, nurturing relationships, and making a lasting impact on the world. At its core, however, living an extraordinary life is about unlocking your potential, pushing past limitations, and embracing a lifestyle that is rich in purpose, joy, and growth. It involves living with intention and breaking free from the patterns that often keep people stuck in ordinary, uninspired lives.

This book is designed to help readers break out of mediocrity, challenge the status quo, and build lives that are extraordinary in their own unique ways. Whether your goals involve personal development, financial independence, improved relationships, or simply more happiness and meaning, this book will provide the tools, insights, and mindset shifts needed to achieve them.

What Does It Mean to Live an Extraordinary Life?

Living an extraordinary life is about reaching beyond the ordinary experiences that most people settle for. It's not about perfection or about having everything figured out, but about continually striving to grow, evolve, and live authentically.

An extraordinary life is one filled with purpose. It's waking up each day with a sense of direction, knowing what drives you and what gives your life meaning. Purpose fuels your actions and decisions, helping you prioritize what's truly important. Whether it's finding meaning in your career, contributing to your community, or building deep personal relationships, living with purpose helps create a sense of fulfillment.

Additionally, an extraordinary life is characterized by balance. Many people think that achieving success means sacrificing their health, relationships, or well-being. However, true success comes from creating harmony in all areas of life. It's about nurturing your physical, mental, emotional, and spiritual health while also striving toward your goals.

Lastly, an extraordinary life is one that is aligned with your values and passions. When you live according to what matters most to you, life feels more vibrant and fulfilling. It's about embracing your uniqueness, pursuing what lights you up, and letting go of societal expectations that don't serve you.

The Myth of the "Perfect Life"

Many people believe that in order to live an extraordinary life, they must have a "perfect life" where everything always goes right. This is a dangerous myth that can create feelings of inadequacy, frustration, and disappointment. Perfection is not only impossible, but it's also unnecessary for living a life filled with meaning and joy.

Perfectionism often leads people to believe that they must avoid making mistakes or experiencing setbacks. They feel that every aspect of their life—career, relationships, appearance—must be flawless to be extraordinary. However, the truth is that mistakes and challenges are a part of the journey. They provide valuable lessons, build resilience, and help you grow. A life without challenges would be flat and unfulfilling.

The myth of the "perfect life" also causes people to focus on external validation, such as wealth, status, or social approval, believing that these things will make them happy. While achieving external success can be rewarding, it doesn't necessarily lead to deep satisfaction. True fulfillment comes from within and is based on personal growth, connections, and contribution rather than from external achievements.

Instead of striving for perfection, focus on progress. Living an extraordinary life means accepting imperfection, learning from failures, and constantly evolving. It's not about having everything in place; it's about being on a journey toward a better version of yourself.

Why Most People Settle for Mediocrity

Many people settle for a life of mediocrity, not because they lack potential, but because they don't believe they can achieve more. There are several reasons why this happens:

1. **Fear of Failure:** Fear is one of the biggest obstacles to living an extraordinary life. People often hold themselves back because they're afraid of making mistakes, being judged, or facing rejection. This fear keeps them in their comfort zones, preventing them from taking risks or pursuing bigger dreams. However, failure is an inevitable part of success. The most extraordinary people are those

who've failed many times but learned from each failure and used it as a stepping stone to greatness.

2. **Lack of Clarity:** Many people aren't clear about what they want from life. They go through the motions, following societal expectations or the paths laid out by others. Without a clear sense of purpose or direction, it's easy to fall into routines that don't bring joy or fulfillment. Having a strong sense of purpose is key to living an extraordinary life, as it provides the motivation and clarity needed to move forward.

3. **Limiting Beliefs:** Negative thoughts about one's abilities and worth often hold people back. Limiting beliefs like "I'm not good

enough" or "I don't deserve success" create mental barriers that prevent individuals from pursuing their full potential. These beliefs are often formed early in life and reinforced over time, making it difficult for people to see beyond them.

4. **Comfort Zones:** It's easy to become comfortable in routines and habits, even if they're not particularly fulfilling. Stepping outside of your comfort zone can be scary, but it's necessary for growth. Most people settle for mediocrity because they prefer the security of the familiar over the uncertainty that comes with pursuing something greater.

5. **External Pressure:** Society often sends messages that suggest people should follow certain conventional paths—get a stable job, buy a house, and settle down. While these can be important milestones, they may not align with everyone's definition of an extraordinary life. External pressure to conform can make it hard for individuals to pursue their unique desires or dreams.

The Roadmap to an Extraordinary Life

Living an extraordinary life doesn't happen by chance—it requires intention, effort, and a clear roadmap. The journey to an extraordinary life involves several key steps:

1. **Self-Awareness:** The first step is to understand who you are and

what you truly want from life. Take the time to reflect on your values, strengths, passions, and desires. Self-awareness allows you to align your actions with your authentic self, rather than following what society expects of you.

2. **Mindset Shift:** Developing a growth mindset is crucial to living an extraordinary life. Believe that you can evolve, improve, and achieve your goals. Shift your thinking from a focus on limitations to a focus on possibilities. This mindset allows you to take risks, learn from failures, and continuously improve.

3. **Setting Clear Goals:** Once you're clear on what you want, it's essential to set specific, measurable

goals. These goals should align with your purpose and values, and they should push you out of your comfort zone. Break your goals into manageable steps, and track your progress along the way.

4. **Developing Habits:** Extraordinary lives are built on the foundation of consistent daily actions. Developing positive habits in areas like health, productivity, and relationships will help you make steady progress toward your goals. Habits create structure and momentum, ensuring that you continue to move forward, even on challenging days.

5. **Building Resilience:** Life will throw challenges and obstacles your way, but resilience allows you to navigate these with grace and

strength. Building emotional and mental toughness will help you stay focused and determined, even in difficult times. Embrace adversity as part of your journey and use it as an opportunity for growth.

6. **Nurturing Relationships:** Relationships play a critical role in living an extraordinary life. Surround yourself with people who inspire, support, and challenge you to be your best self. Build deep, meaningful connections, and contribute positively to the lives of others. Relationships provide emotional fulfillment and create a sense of belonging.

7. **Finding Balance:** An extraordinary life is not just about achievement; it's about balance. Pay attention to

all areas of your life—health, relationships, career, and personal growth. Don't sacrifice one area in the pursuit of another. Strive for harmony, so you can experience success without feeling burnt out or disconnected.

By following this roadmap, you can begin to live an extraordinary life that is rich in purpose, fulfillment, and joy. This path may not always be easy, but the rewards are well worth the effort. Embrace the journey, and remember that an extraordinary life is not about perfection—it's about progress and purpose.

PART 1
MINDSET MASTERY

The foundation of living an extraordinary life begins with mastering your mindset. Your thoughts and beliefs shape your reality, and the way you perceive challenges, opportunities, and yourself determines your success. Many people overlook the power of their mindset, but it is the key to unlocking your potential. When you develop a mindset focused on growth, resilience, and self-awareness, you give yourself the tools needed to achieve greatness and live a fulfilling life.

The Power of Belief
Belief is a powerful force that influences every area of your life. What you believe

about yourself, others, and the world directly affects your actions and decisions. If you believe you are capable of achieving great things, you will approach life with confidence, determination, and focus. On the other hand, if you believe you're not good enough or destined to fail, you'll hold yourself back, missing out on opportunities.

The power of belief lies in its ability to shape your behavior. When you believe in your potential, you are more likely to take risks, push past obstacles, and work toward your goals, even when the road gets tough. Belief fuels your motivation and keeps you moving forward. It also helps you stay resilient in the face of failure because you trust that setbacks are temporary and part of the learning process.

To live an extraordinary life, you must cultivate empowering beliefs. You need to believe in your ability to grow, adapt, and overcome challenges. This is where mindset mastery begins—by transforming your beliefs into ones that propel you forward rather than hold you back.

The Science Behind Mindset

Research shows that mindset plays a significant role in how people respond to challenges and opportunities. Psychologist Carol Dweck's groundbreaking work on "fixed" and "growth" mindsets reveals how our perception of our abilities shapes our behavior. People with a fixed mindset believe their abilities and intelligence are static—they cannot change or improve. As a result, they avoid challenges, fear failure, and shy away from learning new things.

In contrast, people with a growth mindset believe that abilities can be developed through effort, learning, and perseverance. They see challenges as opportunities to grow and view failure as a necessary step toward improvement. This mindset leads to greater resilience, creativity, and success because individuals with a growth mindset are not afraid to take risks and learn from their mistakes.

Understanding the science behind mindset shows that your abilities are not set in stone. You have the power to improve, learn, and grow, no matter where you are in life. By adopting a growth mindset, you open yourself up to new possibilities and empower yourself to live an extraordinary life.

How to Rewire Your Thoughts for Success

Rewiring your thoughts for success is a process that involves changing negative or limiting beliefs and replacing them with positive, empowering ones. This process begins with becoming aware of the thoughts that run through your mind on a daily basis. Many people operate on autopilot, not realizing that their thoughts are holding them back.

Start by paying attention to your inner dialogue. Are you constantly doubting yourself? Do you focus on what could go wrong instead of what could go right? Are you afraid to take action because you fear failure? Once you identify these negative thought patterns, you can begin to challenge and replace them.

One effective technique is to practice positive affirmations. These are statements that reinforce your belief in your abilities and potential. For example, instead of thinking, "I can't do this," you can say, "I am capable of learning and achieving this goal." Repeating positive affirmations helps train your mind to focus on what is possible rather than what is limiting.

Another way to rewire your thoughts is by practicing gratitude. When you focus on what you're grateful for, you shift your attention away from negative thoughts and toward positivity. Gratitude helps you appreciate the progress you've made and reinforces the belief that good things are possible. Over time, these practices will help you cultivate a mindset that supports success and personal growth.

Overcoming Limiting Beliefs
Limiting beliefs are deeply ingrained thoughts that tell you what you can or

cannot do. These beliefs often stem from past experiences, societal expectations, or the opinions of others. For example, you might believe that you're not smart enough to succeed, that success is only for certain types of people, or that you don't deserve happiness. These beliefs can hold you back from pursuing your dreams and living an extraordinary life.

The first step in overcoming limiting beliefs is to recognize them. Reflect on areas of your life where you feel stuck or unfulfilled. Ask yourself, "What belief is keeping me from moving forward?" Once you've identified the limiting belief, challenge its validity. Is there evidence to support this belief, or is it based on fear or past failures?

Next, replace the limiting belief with an empowering one. For example, if you believe you're not good enough, replace that with the belief that you are constantly improving and learning. Reinforce this new belief through action—take small steps that prove to yourself that you are capable. Over time, as you see results, the limiting belief will lose its power, and you'll begin to operate from a place of confidence and possibility.

Identifying Your Self-Imposed Barriers

Self-imposed barriers are the obstacles you unknowingly create for yourself. These barriers often manifest as excuses, procrastination, or self-doubt, and they prevent you from reaching your full potential. For example, you might convince yourself that you don't have enough time to pursue your goals or that you're too old to make a change in your life.

To identify your self-imposed barriers, ask yourself where you've been holding back. Are there areas of your life where you've made excuses instead of taking action? What fears or doubts are keeping you from stepping outside of your comfort zone? Once you've identified these barriers, you can begin to dismantle them.

The key to breaking free from self-imposed barriers is to take responsibility for your life. Acknowledge that while external circumstances may influence your situation, you have the power to change your mindset and actions. By taking ownership of your choices, you empower yourself to remove the barriers standing in your way.

Strategies to Break Free
Breaking free from limiting beliefs and self-imposed barriers requires a

combination of mindset shifts and practical strategies. One effective strategy is to set small, achievable goals. These goals help build momentum and give you a sense of accomplishment, which boosts your confidence. As you achieve each goal, you'll begin to see that you're capable of more than you previously thought.

Another strategy is to surround yourself with supportive people. The people in your life can either uplift or hold you back. Seek out individuals who encourage your growth, challenge you to be better, and believe in your potential. Their positive influence will help reinforce your belief in yourself and push you to break free from limitations.

Lastly, take action. The longer you wait to address your limiting beliefs, the more powerful they become. Even small steps toward your goals can make a difference. Action creates momentum, and momentum helps you overcome barriers that once seemed insurmountable.

Building Resilience

Resilience is the ability to bounce back from adversity, challenges, and setbacks. It's an essential skill for anyone who wants to live an extraordinary life because the path to success is rarely smooth. Building resilience allows you to stay focused on your goals, even when things don't go as planned.

Resilience is developed through experience. Every time you face a challenge and come out stronger, you build resilience. It's about learning how to navigate obstacles without letting them derail your progress. This means accepting that failure is a natural part of growth and using it as an opportunity to learn and improve.

How to Embrace Failure as a Stepping Stone

Failure is inevitable when you're striving for greatness, but how you respond to failure determines your success. Instead of seeing failure as the end, view it as a stepping stone to something greater. Each failure brings valuable lessons about what works and what doesn't, helping you refine your approach and improve over time.

To embrace failure, shift your mindset from "failure is bad" to "failure is part of the process." When you fail, take time to reflect on what went wrong and what you can do differently next time. This reflection helps you grow and ensures that you're constantly moving forward.

Developing Emotional and Mental Toughness

Emotional and mental toughness are critical for navigating life's challenges. Emotional toughness means being able to manage your emotions in stressful situations, while mental toughness is about maintaining focus and determination, even when the going gets tough. Both are essential for overcoming obstacles and achieving long-term success.

To develop emotional toughness, practice mindfulness and self-regulation. This involves becoming aware of your emotional triggers and learning how to respond to them in a calm, constructive way. Developing mental toughness involves setting clear goals, staying disciplined, and pushing through discomfort. Both skills require practice, but over time, they will help you face adversity with confidence and strength.

The Importance of Self-Awareness

Self-awareness is the cornerstone of personal growth. It involves understanding your strengths, weaknesses, values, and motivations. When you're self-aware, you can make choices that align with who you truly are, rather than being influenced by external factors or societal expectations.

To become more self-aware, regularly reflect on your actions, thoughts, and feelings. Ask yourself, "Why did I react that way?" or "What is driving my behavior in this situation?" This introspection helps you uncover patterns and habits that may be holding you back. It also allows you to make intentional decisions that support your growth and happiness.

Understanding Your Strengths and Weaknesses

Understanding your strengths allows you to leverage them for success. When you know what you're good at, you can focus your energy on activities that bring you joy and fulfillment. At the same time, understanding your weaknesses helps you identify areas where you need improvement or support.

Don't view weaknesses as flaws; instead, see them as opportunities for growth. By acknowledging your weaknesses, you can either work to improve them or delegate tasks that don't align with your strengths. This balanced approach ensures that you're maximizing your potential while continuously growing.

Creating a Personal Growth Plan

A personal growth plan is a roadmap for achieving your goals and becoming the best version of yourself. It involves setting specific, actionable goals that align with your values and desires. Your growth plan should include short-term and long-term goals, as well as the steps you'll take to achieve them.

To create a personal growth plan, start by identifying the areas of your life where you want to improve. These could include your career, relationships, health, or personal development. Set clear, measurable goals in each area, and break them down into manageable steps. Regularly review and adjust your plan as you make progress, ensuring that it continues to align with your evolving goals and aspirations.

A well-structured personal growth plan will help you stay focused, motivated, and accountable as you work toward living an extraordinary life.

PART 2

PURPOSE AND PASSION

Purpose and passion are the driving forces behind an extraordinary life. Without purpose, it's easy to drift through life, unsure of why you do what you do. Without passion, life can feel uninspired and dull. But when you discover what gives your life meaning and align your actions with that purpose, everything changes. You feel more alive, motivated, and fulfilled. Purpose and passion are what separate ordinary living from extraordinary living.

Discovering Your Purpose
Finding your purpose is one of the most important steps toward living an extraordinary life. Purpose is the "why" behind your actions, the reason you get out of bed in the morning, and the driving

force behind your goals. It gives your life direction and helps you navigate challenges with a sense of clarity.

Discovering your purpose begins with self-reflection. Ask yourself, "What makes me feel alive? What do I care deeply about? What impact do I want to make in the world?" Your purpose doesn't have to be something grand or world-changing. It could be as simple as raising a family, helping others in your community, or creating art that brings joy to people's lives. The key is to find what feels meaningful to you.

One way to discover your purpose is to reflect on past experiences where you felt most fulfilled. What activities or moments brought you a sense of joy, accomplishment, or peace? These experiences can give you clues about your deeper purpose. Additionally, consider the values that matter most to you—whether it's kindness, creativity, freedom, or connection—and think about how these values can shape your purpose.

How to Find What Truly Drives You

To find what truly drives you, it's essential to explore your interests, passions, and values. What excites you? What topics or activities do you find yourself thinking about or engaging in, even when no one is watching? The things that consistently capture your attention and energize you often point to what drives you.

A useful exercise is to list the things that make you happy or feel fulfilled. Think about your hobbies, work, and relationships, and identify which aspects of these areas bring you the most joy or satisfaction. Pay attention to what activities give you a sense of "flow"—those moments when you're so immersed in what you're doing that time seems to fly by.

Once you've identified the things that drive you, the next step is to align them with your purpose. Ask yourself how you can incorporate more of these activities into your daily life or use them to make a positive impact on others. When you connect your actions with what truly drives you, you'll experience more motivation and fulfillment in everything you do.

Aligning Your Purpose with Your Actions

Living an extraordinary life requires aligning your purpose with your actions. It's not enough to simply know your purpose; you must also take intentional steps toward living it every day. This means making decisions that reflect your values and goals, even when it's difficult or inconvenient.

To align your purpose with your actions, start by evaluating your current habits and routines. Are they supporting your purpose, or are they taking you off course? For example, if your purpose is to help others, are you dedicating time to volunteering or supporting those around you? If your purpose is to create art, are you making time each day to practice and refine your craft?

Aligning your actions with your purpose also means being mindful of the people you surround yourself with and the environments you choose. Surround yourself with individuals who support your purpose and inspire you to be your best. Avoid situations or relationships that drain your energy or distract you from your goals.

Consistency is key. Even small, daily actions that align with your purpose can have a profound impact on your life. Over time, these actions build momentum and create a sense of fulfillment, helping you live in harmony with your purpose.

The Power of Passion
Passion is what fuels an extraordinary life. It's the fire inside you that drives you to keep going, even when things get tough. When you're passionate about something, you bring energy, enthusiasm, and creativity to everything you do. Passion is what makes life exciting and meaningful.

The power of passion lies in its ability to sustain you through challenges. When you're passionate about your work, a cause, or a personal goal, you're more likely to stay committed, even when obstacles arise. Passion gives you the motivation to push past difficulties because you're doing something that matters to you.

Passion also brings a sense of joy and fulfillment. When you engage in activities you're passionate about, you enter a state of flow where you lose track of time and feel completely immersed in what you're doing. This sense of engagement and enjoyment makes life feel richer and more rewarding.

How Passion Fuels an Extraordinary Life

Passion fuels an extraordinary life by giving you a reason to pursue your dreams with energy and excitement. It transforms ordinary tasks into meaningful experiences and helps you maintain a positive outlook, even in the face of setbacks. Passion drives you to improve, to innovate, and to push the boundaries of what you thought was possible.

When you're passionate about something, it becomes easier to put in the time and effort required to succeed. Whether it's your career, a hobby, or a personal mission, passion helps you stay focused and dedicated. It allows you to approach challenges with creativity and persistence, making it more likely that you'll overcome obstacles and achieve your goals.

Moreover, passion is contagious. When you're passionate about something, others can sense it. Your enthusiasm can inspire and motivate those around you, creating a positive ripple effect that extends beyond your own life. Passion gives you the drive to make a difference and live in a way that impacts others positively.

Overcoming the Fear of Pursuing Your Passion

One of the biggest obstacles to living a passionate and purposeful life is fear—fear of failure, fear of judgment, or fear of the unknown. Many people hold back from pursuing their passions because they're afraid they won't succeed or that others will criticize them. However, overcoming this fear is essential if you want to live an extraordinary life.

The first step in overcoming fear is acknowledging it. Recognize that fear is a natural part of the process of growth and change. Instead of letting fear hold you back, use it as a signal that you're stepping outside of your comfort zone and into a space where real growth happens.

One effective way to overcome the fear of pursuing your passion is to start small. Take small steps toward your passion, and gradually build your confidence. For example, if your passion is writing, start by dedicating 15 minutes a day to writing. Over time, as you become more comfortable and skilled, you can increase your efforts.

Remember that failure is part of the journey. It's better to try and fail than to never try at all. Each failure brings valuable lessons that will help you grow and improve. Embrace the learning process and trust that, with persistence, you'll succeed in pursuing your passion.

Living with Intention

Living with intention means being purposeful and deliberate about how you spend your time and energy. It's about making conscious choices that align with your values and goals, rather than going through life on autopilot. When you live with intention, each day becomes an opportunity to make progress toward your dreams and to live in a way that feels meaningful and fulfilling.

To live with intention, start by setting clear priorities. What matters most to you? What are your long-term goals, and what daily actions can you take to move closer to them? By focusing on your top priorities, you can avoid distractions and make decisions that support your overall purpose.

Intentional living also involves mindfulness. Pay attention to how you're spending your time and whether your actions align with your values. Are you dedicating time to the things that bring you joy and fulfillment, or are you getting caught up in activities that don't serve your purpose? Regularly check in with yourself to ensure that you're living in a way that reflects your true intentions.

How to Make Each Day Meaningful

Making each day meaningful doesn't require grand gestures or significant achievements. It's about finding small moments of joy, connection, and purpose in your everyday life. Start by setting an intention for each day—whether it's to learn something new, to connect with someone, or to make progress on a personal goal.

Gratitude is another powerful tool for creating meaning. Take a few moments each day to reflect on what you're grateful for. Focusing on the positive aspects of your life, no matter how small, can shift your mindset and help you appreciate the present moment.

Additionally, engage in activities that bring you fulfillment. Whether it's spending time with loved ones, pursuing a hobby, or working toward a goal, prioritize the things that make you feel alive and purposeful. By infusing meaning into your daily routine, you'll feel more connected to your purpose and passion.

Creating and Sticking to Life Goals
Setting life goals gives you direction and a sense of purpose. Your goals represent the milestones you want to achieve in various areas of your life, from your career and relationships to your personal growth and well-being. However, setting goals is only the first step. The real challenge lies in sticking to them.

To create meaningful life goals, start by identifying what matters most to you. What do you want to achieve in your lifetime, and why? Make sure your goals align with your purpose and passion, as this will provide the motivation needed to stay committed.

Break your goals down into smaller, manageable steps. Large goals can feel overwhelming, but by breaking them into smaller tasks, you can make steady progress over time. Each step brings you closer to your ultimate goal and gives you a sense of accomplishment.

Accountability is key to sticking to your goals. Share your goals with a friend, mentor, or accountability partner who can encourage you and hold you accountable. Regularly review your progress and adjust your plan as needed. By staying focused and committed, you'll be able to achieve your life goals and live an extraordinary life.

PART 3

HABITS OF HIGH ACHIEVERS

The habits of high achievers are what separate them from the rest. These habits are often simple yet consistent actions that, over time, lead to extraordinary success. By adopting similar routines and mindsets, you can start living an extraordinary life, regardless of where you are right now. High achievers are intentional about how they spend their time, take care of their bodies, and manage their mental and emotional well-being. This section explores the powerful habits that fuel their success and how you can incorporate them into your own life.

The Daily Routines of Extraordinary People

One of the most common traits of high achievers is their dedication to structured routines. Extraordinary people often have a set of daily habits that keep them focused, energized, and productive. Their routines are designed to maximize efficiency while allowing them to stay on top of their goals.

For many high achievers, mornings are sacred. They typically wake up early to take advantage of the quiet hours before the demands of the day begin. This time is often spent on activities that nourish both body and mind, such as exercise, meditation, or reading. By starting the day with intention, they set a positive tone that carries throughout the day.

Beyond the morning, successful individuals often block out specific times for deep work, reflection, and personal growth. They understand the importance of balancing work with rest, and they make time for hobbies, learning, and self-care. Their routines are designed to help them maintain a sense of control over their day while ensuring they make steady progress toward their goals.

How Morning Routines Can Transform Your Life

Morning routines are particularly powerful because they allow you to start your day with purpose and clarity. By incorporating specific habits into your morning, you set the stage for a productive and fulfilling day. High achievers often use their mornings to focus on personal development, fitness, and mental clarity.

For example, many successful individuals begin their mornings with some form of exercise, whether it's a quick workout, a jog, or yoga. Physical activity not only boosts energy but also improves focus and mood, making it easier to tackle the challenges of the day. Another common element of a powerful morning routine is mindfulness—whether through meditation, journaling, or simply setting daily intentions. These practices help center the mind and create a sense of calm before diving into the busyness of life.

A key benefit of a strong morning routine is that it sets the tone for the entire day. When you begin your day with a series of positive habits, you create momentum that carries you through the rest of your tasks. You're more likely to stay focused, make better decisions, and feel accomplished by the end of the day. Even if you don't have hours to dedicate to a morning routine, just 15-30 minutes of intentional activity can make a significant difference.

The Power of Consistency
Consistency is the foundation of success for high achievers. It's not about doing something extraordinary once but rather doing the right things repeatedly, day in and day out. This could mean sticking to a workout routine, maintaining a daily writing habit, or making time for reflection. Small, consistent actions over time lead to significant results.

Consistency allows you to build momentum and gradually improve in any area of life. For example, if you commit to reading for 20 minutes each day, you'll gain knowledge and insights over time that can transform your mindset and abilities. Similarly, a consistent focus on health—whether through exercise, healthy eating, or mindfulness—leads to long-term physical and emotional well-being.

The key to consistency is creating habits that are realistic and sustainable. High achievers don't overwhelm themselves with unrealistic expectations; instead, they set achievable goals and commit to doing them regularly. They understand that progress may be slow at times, but they trust that consistency will yield results.

Mastering Time and Focus

Time management is a crucial skill for high achievers. They are intentional about how they allocate their time, ensuring that their daily activities align with their goals and values. One of the most effective ways to manage time is to prioritize what truly matters and eliminate distractions.

Many high achievers use techniques such as time blocking to structure their day. Time blocking involves setting aside specific periods for focused work, meetings, and personal tasks. By assigning time to each task, they prevent distractions and make the most of each hour. High achievers also recognize the importance of taking breaks to recharge and maintain their focus throughout the day.

Another important aspect of mastering time is knowing when to say "no." High achievers are selective about how they spend their time and energy. They avoid unnecessary commitments and focus on activities that move them closer to their goals. This allows them to maintain a high level of focus and productivity.

Prioritizing What Truly Matters

Living an extraordinary life requires prioritizing the things that matter most to you. High achievers are experts at focusing on their core values and long-term goals, rather than getting sidetracked by immediate but less important tasks. They are constantly asking themselves, "Is this activity moving me toward my goals?"

To prioritize effectively, you must first clarify your long-term objectives. What are the most important things you want to achieve in your life? Once you have a clear vision, break those goals down into actionable steps and ensure that your daily actions align with those steps. By keeping your goals in focus, you'll be able to say no to distractions and stay on the path to success.

Additionally, high achievers prioritize their well-being. They recognize that personal health, relationships, and happiness are just as important as professional success. By balancing work with life's other joys, they create a sense of fulfillment that goes beyond achievements.

Avoiding Distractions and Procrastination

Distractions and procrastination are two of the biggest enemies of productivity. High achievers understand this and develop strategies to avoid them. They create environments that foster focus, such as working in quiet spaces, turning off notifications, and setting clear boundaries around work time.

One of the most effective ways to avoid procrastination is to break large tasks into smaller, more manageable steps. High achievers understand that the overwhelming nature of a big project can often lead to procrastination. By focusing on just one small task at a time, they reduce the urge to put things off and make steady progress.

They also use techniques like the "two-minute rule," which suggests that if a task can be done in two minutes or less, it should be completed immediately. This helps prevent small tasks from piling up and becoming overwhelming. High achievers also set deadlines for themselves, even when no external deadline exists, to create a sense of urgency and accountability.

Health and Wellness for Optimal Living

High achievers know that their physical health plays a crucial role in their success. A healthy body supports a sharp mind, high energy levels, and the stamina needed to pursue big goals. This is why they prioritize physical well-being through regular exercise, proper nutrition, and adequate sleep.

Exercise is often a non-negotiable part of their routine. It helps to boost energy, improve focus, and reduce stress. High achievers are not necessarily athletes, but they understand the importance of staying active, whether it's through daily walks, yoga, or more intense workouts. Consistent movement is essential for maintaining a high level of performance.

Nutrition is another key area. High achievers often pay close attention to what they eat, fueling their bodies with wholesome, nutrient-dense foods. They avoid foods that sap their energy or negatively impact their health, opting instead for meals that keep them alert and focused throughout the day. Hydration also plays an important role, with many high achievers making sure to drink plenty of water to stay hydrated and energized.

Sleep is often a priority, too. While the myth of the "sleepless entrepreneur" persists, most high achievers know that adequate rest is vital for mental clarity, decision-making, and overall well-being. They make sleep a priority by sticking to a regular sleep schedule and creating bedtime routines that promote restful sleep.

Why Physical Health is Non-Negotiable

For high achievers, physical health is not just important—it's non-negotiable. They understand that their bodies are the foundation of everything they do. Without physical health, it's difficult to maintain the focus, energy, and stamina required for success. As such, they prioritize exercise, nutrition, and rest as essential components of their daily lives.

Physical health also contributes to mental clarity. Regular exercise has been shown to improve brain function, reduce stress, and enhance mood. High achievers use physical activity not just to stay fit but also to keep their minds sharp and focused.

In addition, taking care of your body is a form of self-respect. When you invest in your health, you are signaling to yourself and others that you value your well-being. This self-respect can have a ripple effect, boosting confidence and motivation in other areas of life.

Mental and Emotional Wellness Practices

High achievers understand that mental and emotional wellness is just as important as physical health. Success can bring its own set of challenges, including stress, anxiety, and emotional strain. To maintain balance, high achievers regularly engage in practices that support their mental and emotional well-being.

Meditation, mindfulness, and journaling are common practices among high achievers. These activities help them clear their minds, manage stress, and stay connected to their emotions. Meditation, in particular, has been shown to reduce stress and improve focus. High achievers often incorporate a few minutes of meditation into their daily routines to stay grounded and centered.

Emotional wellness also involves cultivating healthy relationships. High achievers prioritize their connections with family, friends, and mentors. They understand that strong relationships provide emotional support, inspiration, and a sense of belonging. By nurturing these relationships, they create a network of support that helps them stay resilient in the face of challenges.

In summary, the habits of high achievers are rooted in consistency, intentionality, and balance. They focus on the things that truly matter, prioritize their health and well-being, and manage their time with purpose. By adopting these habits, you, too, can begin living an extraordinary life.

PART 4

BUILDING MEANINGFUL RELATIONSHIPS

Building meaningful relationships is a cornerstone of living an extraordinary life. The connections we form with others influence our success, happiness, and overall sense of fulfillment. High achievers understand the importance of surrounding themselves with positive, supportive people who encourage growth and well-being. In this section, we'll explore the power of relationships, the art of effective communication, and how empathy and kindness can deepen connections with those around us.

The Power of Positive Relationships

Positive relationships have a profound impact on our lives. They provide us with emotional support, help us grow as individuals, and offer opportunities for collaboration and learning. High achievers recognize that the people they surround themselves with play a critical role in their success. When you have a circle of positive, uplifting individuals, it becomes easier to stay motivated, overcome challenges, and celebrate achievements.

Strong relationships are built on trust, mutual respect, and shared values. These connections create a sense of security and belonging, which allows us to take risks and pursue our goals with confidence. Additionally, positive relationships can inspire us to become better versions of ourselves. Whether through mentorship, friendship, or partnership, the influence of others can push us to grow in ways we might not have been able to on our own.

Surrounding yourself with people who believe in you and your vision creates a supportive environment for personal and professional growth. These relationships act as a safety net during difficult times and as a source of celebration during moments of success.

How Your Circle Influences Your Life

The people we spend the most time with have a significant impact on our mindset, habits, and overall outlook on life. If you surround yourself with negative, critical individuals, you may find yourself feeling drained, unmotivated, and uncertain. On the other hand, a circle of positive, encouraging people can uplift and energize you, helping you stay focused and driven.

Jim Rohn's famous quote, "You are the average of the five people you spend the most time with," highlights the importance of choosing your circle carefully. High achievers understand that their success is often linked to the quality of their relationships. If you want to live an extraordinary life, it's crucial to evaluate who is in your inner circle and whether they are helping or hindering your growth.

Your circle should consist of individuals who challenge you to think bigger, offer constructive feedback, and support you in achieving your goals. At the same time, it's essential to be selective about the energy and values you allow into your life. Surrounding yourself with people who are aligned with your aspirations will help you stay on track and focused on what truly matters.

Building Supportive, Encouraging Connections

Building supportive relationships requires effort, intention, and a genuine desire to connect with others. High achievers prioritize developing meaningful connections with people who encourage their growth, both personally and professionally. They seek out individuals who share similar values and goals, while also being open to learning from those with different perspectives.

One way to build strong connections is by being proactive in seeking out opportunities to meet like-minded people. This might include joining professional networks, attending social events, or simply reaching out to someone you admire. Building connections also requires active listening and a willingness to invest time and energy into relationships.

Supportive relationships are built on mutual respect and trust. When you demonstrate genuine care for others and show up consistently, you create a foundation of trust that leads to deeper, more meaningful connections. In these relationships, both parties benefit from mutual encouragement, advice, and emotional support.

The Art of Effective Communication

Communication is the key to building and maintaining meaningful relationships. High achievers are skilled communicators who understand that how they convey their thoughts and feelings can strengthen or weaken connections with others. Effective communication is about more than just speaking; it involves active listening, empathy, and clarity.

At the core of effective communication is the ability to listen. Too often, conversations become one-sided when people focus solely on sharing their own thoughts without taking the time to understand the other person's perspective. High achievers make a conscious effort to listen actively and attentively, ensuring that they fully understand what others are saying before responding.

Clear communication also involves speaking with purpose. High achievers are deliberate in their choice of words, ensuring that their message is conveyed in a way that is both respectful and impactful. By focusing on clarity, they avoid misunderstandings and ensure that their communication strengthens relationships rather than causing friction.

How to Be a Better Listener

Listening is an underrated skill but is one of the most critical components of effective communication. High achievers know that listening deeply fosters trust and connection in relationships. To be a better listener, it's essential to be fully present during conversations. This means giving the other person your undivided attention, avoiding distractions like your phone or other tasks, and focusing solely on the speaker.

Active listening involves not just hearing the words being said but understanding the emotions and intentions behind them. When someone feels truly heard, they are more likely to trust you and open up, deepening the connection between you. To practice active listening, ask clarifying questions, paraphrase what you've heard, and acknowledge the other person's feelings. This demonstrates that you value their perspective and are engaged in the conversation.

Speaking with Purpose and Clarity

High achievers know the value of speaking with purpose and clarity. Whether in personal or professional settings, being clear in your communication can prevent misunderstandings, build trust, and ensure that your message resonates with others. Speaking with purpose means being intentional about what you say and how you say it.

Before speaking, consider the goal of the conversation. Are you offering advice, seeking to understand, or providing feedback? By understanding your purpose, you can tailor your message to meet the needs of the conversation. Clarity is also essential—use simple, straightforward language, and avoid being vague or ambiguous.

It's also important to be mindful of your tone and body language. Non-verbal cues can communicate just as much as words. High achievers pay attention to how their tone and gestures align with their message, ensuring that their communication is both sincere and respectful.

Developing Empathy and Compassion

Empathy is the ability to understand and share the feelings of others. High achievers understand that empathy is essential for building meaningful relationships because it allows them to connect on a deeper level with the people around them. When you can see the world from someone else's perspective, you're better able to offer support, encouragement, and understanding.

Empathy goes beyond simply putting yourself in someone else's shoes—it involves being genuinely curious about their experiences, emotions, and needs. When you approach conversations with empathy, you create a safe space for others to express themselves openly and honestly. High achievers practice empathy by being fully present in conversations, asking thoughtful questions, and offering non-judgmental support.

Compassion takes empathy a step further by motivating us to take action. When you see someone struggling, compassion drives you to offer help or support. Developing compassion strengthens relationships because it shows others that you genuinely care about their well-being.

How Empathy Leads to Better Relationships

Empathy is a powerful tool for strengthening relationships. When you demonstrate empathy, you build trust, foster emotional intimacy, and create a sense of mutual understanding. High achievers use empathy to connect with others on a deeper level, creating relationships that are both supportive and fulfilling.

Empathy allows you to navigate difficult conversations with grace and understanding. Instead of reacting defensively or judgmentally, you're able to listen and respond in a way that acknowledges the other person's feelings. This can prevent conflicts from escalating and help resolve issues in a positive, constructive manner.

Empathy also helps you be a better leader and team member. In professional settings, high achievers use empathy to understand the needs and concerns of their colleagues, which leads to better collaboration and problem-solving. In personal relationships, empathy helps you be more patient, supportive, and understanding of the challenges others face.

The Ripple Effect of Kindness

Kindness is a simple yet powerful way to enhance relationships. High achievers understand that acts of kindness, no matter how small, can have a lasting impact on the people around them. When you treat others with kindness, you create a ripple effect that spreads positivity and encourages others to do the same.

Kindness fosters goodwill and trust in relationships. Whether it's offering a word of encouragement, helping someone in need, or simply being polite and respectful, acts of kindness show others that you care. Over time, these small gestures build strong, meaningful connections.

The ripple effect of kindness extends beyond individual relationships. When you practice kindness, you contribute to a culture of compassion and respect. This not only strengthens your personal relationships but also creates a positive environment in your community and workplace.

In conclusion, building meaningful relationships requires intentionality, effective communication, empathy, and kindness. High achievers prioritize their relationships, recognizing that the quality of their connections significantly impacts their personal and professional success. By developing supportive relationships, practicing active listening, and showing empathy and kindness, you can create a network of meaningful connections that enrich your life and help you live more extraordinarily.

PART 5

OVERCOMING CHALLENGES

Living an extraordinary life doesn't mean avoiding difficulties or never encountering problems. In fact, the way we face challenges often defines how extraordinary our lives can be. Challenges test our resolve, push us to grow, and show us what we're truly capable of. In this section, we will dive deeply into how to overcome adversity, develop resilience, and navigate through life's tough moments while maintaining a sense of peace and direction.

Facing Adversity with Courage
Courage is not the absence of fear but the ability to move forward despite it. Life throws unexpected situations our way—be it loss, failure, or setbacks—and what

distinguishes high achievers is their ability to face these adversities head-on. Courage is essential because it allows you to act even when the outcome is uncertain or when the path ahead is difficult.

When faced with adversity, it's important to acknowledge your fears and doubts without letting them dictate your actions. Rather than avoiding or denying tough situations, courageous individuals confront them with honesty and a willingness to find solutions. The key is to remind yourself that challenges are temporary and that with persistence, you can overcome them.

Courage also means accepting that not everything will go as planned. Sometimes, you may not have control over external circumstances, but you always have control over how you respond. Taking responsibility for your reactions and choosing to act with bravery in the face of uncertainty is a crucial step toward overcoming adversity.

Why Hard Times Are Crucial for Growth

Hard times are often seen as obstacles, but they are actually opportunities for growth. In moments of struggle, we learn the most about ourselves—our strengths, weaknesses, and what truly matters to us. Challenges force us to step out of our comfort zones, try new approaches, and develop skills we never knew we needed.

Adversity builds resilience. It teaches you how to bounce back from setbacks and helps you develop mental and emotional toughness. Each time you face and overcome a challenge, you build confidence in your ability to handle future difficulties. This sense of self-assurance becomes a driving force that propels you forward, even when the road gets tough.

Hard times also provide valuable lessons. They teach us patience, perseverance, and problem-solving. Many successful individuals can point to moments of failure or hardship as pivotal times in their journey where they learned critical lessons that contributed to their future success. By viewing challenges as learning experiences, you can turn obstacles into stepping stones.

Strategies to Handle Life's Setbacks

Everyone faces setbacks, but how you handle them determines whether they derail your progress or become part of your growth journey. One effective strategy for handling setbacks is to adopt a mindset of flexibility. When things don't go according to plan, instead of feeling defeated, look for ways to adjust your approach and keep moving forward. Flexibility allows you to adapt to changing circumstances and find new solutions.

Another important strategy is maintaining perspective. Setbacks can feel overwhelming in the moment, but it's important to step back and evaluate the situation objectively. Ask yourself: Is this setback temporary or permanent? What can I learn from this? By focusing on the bigger picture, you'll realize that most setbacks are simply bumps in the road, not dead ends.

Lastly, surround yourself with a support system. Whether it's friends, family, or mentors, having people you trust to offer advice and encouragement can make a significant difference when facing difficulties. Sometimes, a fresh perspective from someone outside the situation can help you see solutions that you might have missed.

Developing a Problem-Solving Mindset

A problem-solving mindset is key to navigating challenges effectively. High achievers approach problems not with a sense of defeat, but with a determination to find solutions. This mindset involves staying calm, assessing the situation logically, and exploring all possible options.

The first step to developing a problem-solving mindset is to break down the issue into manageable parts. Rather than getting overwhelmed by the entirety of a problem, focus on one aspect at a time. This makes the problem less daunting and allows you to tackle it step by step.

Next, it's important to be creative and open-minded when looking for solutions. Often, the best solutions come from thinking outside the box or approaching a problem from a different angle. Don't be afraid to try unconventional approaches if traditional methods aren't working.

Lastly, high achievers understand that not every problem has a perfect solution, and that's okay. Sometimes, the goal isn't to eliminate the problem entirely but to manage it in a way that minimizes its impact on your life.

How to Navigate Difficult Decisions

Making difficult decisions is an inevitable part of life, especially when pursuing an extraordinary path. These decisions can feel overwhelming because they often involve trade-offs, uncertainty, or the potential for significant consequences. To navigate these tough choices, it's essential to approach them with clarity and confidence.

First, gather as much information as possible. The more informed you are, the easier it is to weigh the pros and cons of each option. Once you have the facts, take time to reflect on your values and long-term goals. Ask yourself: Which choice aligns most closely with the life I want to create? High achievers make decisions that reflect their values and vision, even if those choices are difficult in the short term.

It's also helpful to consult trusted mentors or advisors. They can offer insights or perspectives that you may not have considered. However, remember that the final decision is yours to make. Trust your instincts and believe in your ability to make the best choice for your situation.

Staying Calm Under Pressure
Staying calm under pressure is a crucial skill for overcoming challenges. High achievers remain composed in stressful situations, allowing them to think clearly and make sound decisions. While pressure can create anxiety, learning how to manage it effectively helps you stay in control and handle tough situations with grace.

One technique to stay calm under pressure is to focus on your breathing. Deep, slow breaths can help calm your nervous system and reduce feelings of anxiety. Taking a few moments to breathe and center yourself can make a significant difference in how you approach a stressful situation.

Another important practice is to keep your focus on the present moment. Anxiety often arises when we worry about the future or dwell on past mistakes. By staying grounded in the present, you can better concentrate on what needs to be done right now.

Finally, high achievers maintain perspective under pressure. They remind themselves that pressure is a normal part of life and that they have the skills and resilience to handle it. This mindset shift can turn pressure from a source of stress into a source of motivation.

Managing Stress and Burnout

Stress and burnout are common challenges, especially for those striving for extraordinary achievements. However, managing stress effectively is essential for maintaining long-term success and well-being. Burnout occurs when prolonged stress goes unmanaged, leading to exhaustion and a loss of motivation. To avoid burnout, it's important to recognize the signs of stress early and take proactive steps to address it.

One effective way to manage stress is to prioritize self-care. Taking time for activities that relax and recharge you—whether it's exercise, hobbies, or spending time with loved ones—helps you maintain balance and prevent burnout. Self-care isn't a luxury; it's a necessity for sustaining high performance over the long term.

It's also helpful to set boundaries. High achievers know when to say no to additional responsibilities or commitments that could overwhelm them. By managing your time and energy wisely, you can reduce stress and focus on what truly matters.

Techniques to Protect Your Mental Health

Protecting your mental health is crucial for overcoming challenges and living an extraordinary life. Mental health is often neglected in the pursuit of success, but it's the foundation upon which everything else is built. Without strong mental well-being, it's difficult to sustain the energy, focus, and resilience needed to achieve great things.

One technique to protect your mental health is practicing mindfulness. Mindfulness involves being fully present in the moment and observing your thoughts without judgment. Regular mindfulness practice can help reduce stress, improve focus, and enhance emotional regulation.

Another important technique is to create a support network. Surround yourself with people who understand your struggles and can offer encouragement, whether it's friends, family, or professional counselors. Having someone to talk to when things get tough can make all the difference in maintaining mental well-being.

Finally, recognize when you need a break. Pushing yourself too hard without rest can lead to burnout and mental exhaustion. Taking time to step back, reflect, and recharge is essential for long-term success and happiness.

Recognizing the Signs and Taking Action

Recognizing the signs of stress, burnout, or declining mental health is the first step to taking action. Signs of burnout might include constant fatigue, loss of motivation, feelings of hopelessness, or difficulty concentrating. When you notice these signs, it's essential to address them before they escalate.

Taking action might involve seeking professional help, such as speaking with a therapist or counselor. It could also mean making changes to your routine, such as reducing your workload, taking more breaks, or incorporating stress-relief activities into your daily life.

High achievers know that taking care of their mental and emotional well-being is just as important as achieving their goals. By recognizing when you need help and being proactive about protecting your mental health, you can ensure that you're equipped to face challenges with strength and resilience.

In conclusion, overcoming challenges is a vital part of the journey to living an extraordinary life. Whether it's facing adversity, developing a problem-solving mindset, or managing stress and burnout, the key is to approach challenges with courage, resilience, and a focus on personal growth. By doing so, you'll not only overcome life's obstacles but also emerge stronger, wiser, and more prepared for future success.

PART 6

FINANCIAL FREEDOM AND INDEPENDENCE

Achieving financial freedom and independence is a crucial component of living an extraordinary life. It gives you the flexibility to pursue your passions, enjoy more freedom, and create opportunities for yourself and those around you. This part will explore how mindset, planning, and smart financial decisions can lead to long-term wealth and a life free from financial constraints.

The Mindset of Wealth

Financial success starts in the mind. The way you think about money plays a significant role in how you manage and grow it. People who achieve financial freedom understand the importance of having a wealth-building mindset. This doesn't mean being obsessed with money but rather having a healthy relationship with it. A wealth mindset involves seeing money as a tool for freedom and opportunities, rather than just a necessity for survival.

People with a wealth mindset view financial growth as a possibility for anyone, regardless of their starting point. They understand that with the right habits and discipline, they can build wealth over time. This mindset is optimistic and focused on long-term gains rather than short-term gratification.

A key part of developing a wealth mindset is focusing on value rather than cost. Instead of thinking about how much something costs, think about the value it brings. For example, investing in education or personal growth may have a high upfront cost, but the long-term value it brings to your career and financial well-being can far outweigh the initial investment.

How Financial Success Relates to an Extraordinary Life

Financial success isn't just about having more money; it's about creating a life of choice and freedom. When you have financial stability, you're free to make decisions based on what you truly want, not just what you can afford. This might mean pursuing a passion project, traveling the world, or spending more time with your family. The ultimate goal of financial independence is to live life on your terms.

Financial success allows you to focus on the things that truly matter in life. It removes the stress and limitations that often come with financial instability, giving you the mental and emotional space to focus on personal growth, meaningful relationships, and purposeful living. In many ways, financial freedom is a foundation that supports all other aspects of an extraordinary life.

Another benefit of financial success is the ability to give back. Once you're financially secure, you can contribute to causes that matter to you, help others achieve their goals, and make a positive impact on the world. Living an extraordinary life often involves using your resources to lift others up, and financial freedom gives you the power to do so.

Shifting to an Abundance Mentality

An abundance mentality is crucial for achieving financial independence. This mindset is based on the belief that there are enough resources, opportunities, and wealth to go around, and that your success does not come at the expense of others. In contrast to a scarcity mindset—which sees life as a zero-sum game—an abundance mentality is open to new possibilities and encourages growth.

Shifting to an abundance mentality requires changing the way you think about money. Instead of focusing on lack or limitations, focus on the opportunities around you. This shift in thinking opens you up to new ways of earning, saving, and investing, as well as building wealth.

The abundance mentality also helps reduce financial anxiety. Instead of worrying about what you don't have, you focus on what you can create and achieve. This positive mindset leads to better financial decisions because you're not acting out of fear but out of confidence and optimism. Over time, this shift in thinking can have a profound effect on your financial future.

Building Long-Term Wealth

Building long-term wealth requires patience, discipline, and strategic decision-making. Unlike short-term gains, which can be fleeting, long-term wealth focuses on sustainable growth over time. The first step in building wealth is to have a clear plan and set specific financial goals. Whether your goal is to buy a home, retire early, or start a business, having a roadmap will help you stay on track.

Saving is a crucial component of long-term wealth-building. A disciplined approach to saving ensures that you have a financial cushion for emergencies and are prepared for future opportunities. It's important to live below your means and prioritize saving a portion of your income, even if it's a small amount at first. Over time, consistent saving habits will accumulate and provide you with a solid foundation for financial independence.

Investing is another essential strategy for growing wealth. Investing allows your money to work for you, generating returns over time. Whether it's in stocks, real estate, or other assets, the key is to make smart investments that align with your risk tolerance and financial goals. Diversifying your investments helps mitigate risk and ensures that your wealth is spread across different areas, reducing the impact of market fluctuations.

Lastly, building wealth requires time and patience. It's important to avoid get-rich-quick schemes or high-risk ventures that promise fast returns. True wealth-building is a slow and steady process that requires careful planning and long-term thinking. By sticking to your plan and making informed decisions, you can build lasting wealth that supports your extraordinary life.

Strategies for Saving, Investing, and Growing Your Finances

To achieve financial independence, you need to adopt smart strategies for saving, investing, and growing your finances. One of the most effective strategies for saving is the *pay yourself first* method. This means prioritizing saving a portion of your income before spending on anything else. By automatically setting aside money for savings and investments, you ensure that your financial goals are always a top priority.

Investing in a diverse range of assets is also key to growing your finances. Whether you choose to invest in the stock market, real estate, or business ventures, diversification reduces risk and increases the likelihood of steady growth. It's important to educate yourself about different types of investments and seek advice from financial experts if needed.

Another important strategy is to minimize debt. While some debt, such as a mortgage or student loans, can be considered an investment in your future, high-interest consumer debt can quickly become a financial burden. Paying off debt as quickly as possible frees up your resources to invest and save, accelerating your path to financial independence.

Finally, continuously educating yourself about personal finance is crucial. The world of finance is constantly evolving, and staying informed about new opportunities, tax laws, and investment strategies can help you make better decisions. Financial literacy empowers you to take control of your financial future and make choices that align with your goals.

Escaping the Rat Race

The rat race refers to the endless cycle of working long hours in a job you may not love just to make ends meet. For many people, the pursuit of financial independence is about breaking free from this cycle and creating a life of freedom and flexibility. Escaping the rat race doesn't necessarily mean quitting your job immediately; it means designing a life where you have more control over your time and financial destiny.

One way to escape the rat race is by developing multiple streams of income. Relying on a single source of income can leave you vulnerable to job loss or financial instability. By creating side businesses, passive income streams, or investing in assets that generate income, you can reduce your dependence on a traditional 9-to-5 job.

Financial independence also means living on your own terms. Instead of being tied to a specific job or location, you have the freedom to work when and where you want. This could mean pursuing freelance work, starting your own business, or achieving early retirement. The key is to align your work with your passions and values so that you're not simply working for a paycheck but creating a life that fulfills you.

How to Design a Life of Freedom and Flexibility

Designing a life of freedom and flexibility requires intentional planning and a commitment to financial discipline. Start by defining what freedom and flexibility mean to you. For some, it might mean being able to travel the world without financial constraints. For others, it might mean having the ability to retire early or spend more time with family. Whatever your vision of freedom, it's important to set clear financial goals that will allow you to achieve it.

A critical part of designing this life is prioritizing passive income. Passive income allows you to earn money with minimal effort, freeing up your time for other pursuits. Whether it's through investments, rental properties, or online businesses, creating passive income streams gives you the financial flexibility to focus on what truly matters to you.

Lastly, building a life of freedom involves making intentional choices about how you spend your time and money. It's important to align your financial decisions with your long-term goals. Instead of spending money on things that don't add value to your life, focus on investments that will bring you closer to your vision of financial freedom. By being strategic and disciplined, you can create a life where you have the freedom to pursue your passions, enjoy meaningful experiences, and live with purpose.

Financial freedom and independence are vital components of living an extraordinary life. By adopting a wealth mindset, building long-term wealth, and designing a life of freedom and flexibility, you can create a future where you are in control of your financial destiny. The journey to financial independence may require discipline and hard work, but the rewards are well worth the effort.

PART 7

LEAVING A LASTING LEGACY

Leaving a lasting legacy is about more than what you accomplish during your lifetime—it's about the impact you leave behind, the lives you touch, and how you are remembered long after you're gone. Whether it's through the people you help, the lessons you teach, or the values you instill, creating a legacy is an essential part of living an extraordinary life.

The Importance of Giving Back
At the heart of a lasting legacy is the act of giving back. It's about using your time, resources, and abilities to make a positive difference in the lives of others. Giving back doesn't necessarily mean grand gestures or massive charitable donations; it can be as simple as helping a friend,

mentoring a young person, or volunteering in your community.

The importance of giving back lies in its ability to create a ripple effect. When you help one person, you inspire them to help someone else, and so on. Your contribution multiplies, extending far beyond what you might see in your lifetime. This chain reaction of kindness and generosity can have a lasting impact on communities, organizations, and even future generations.

Giving back also brings personal fulfillment. Many people find that the act of contributing to the well-being of others gives them a deep sense of purpose and satisfaction. It shifts the focus from personal achievement to collective well-being, making life more meaningful and enriching.

How Contribution Leads to Fulfillment

Contribution is one of the key drivers of happiness and fulfillment. While achieving personal goals and experiencing success can bring joy, the feeling of making a positive difference in the world is often more rewarding. Helping others creates a sense of connection, purpose, and belonging that can't be found in personal accomplishments alone.

There's a deep sense of satisfaction in knowing that your efforts have improved someone's life, whether that's through direct assistance, sharing knowledge, or inspiring others to take positive actions. It also fosters gratitude. When you give, you realize how fortunate you are to be in a position to help others, which can put your own challenges into perspective.

Moreover, contribution shifts your focus from inward (your own needs and desires) to outward (the needs of others). This outward focus reduces stress, anxiety, and feelings of isolation, as you become more connected to the broader human experience. It's not just about what you receive, but about the impact you leave behind.

Finding Causes that Align with Your Values

To create a legacy that feels authentic, it's essential to find causes that resonate deeply with your personal values. This alignment ensures that your contributions come from a place of passion and purpose, rather than obligation. When you care deeply about a cause, your commitment is more genuine, and the impact you make is more profound.

The first step is to reflect on what matters most to you. Is it education, environmental sustainability, poverty alleviation, or healthcare? Once you've identified your core values, seek out causes and organizations that share your vision. It could be through charity work, advocacy, or even starting your own initiative. Aligning your efforts with your passions ensures that your contribution is meaningful and lasting.

For example, if education is something you value, you might support initiatives that provide scholarships for underprivileged students or mentor young people in your field of expertise. If environmental sustainability resonates with you, perhaps you'll work on projects that promote conservation or reduce waste. The key is to focus on areas where you can make a meaningful difference, and that reflect your values.

Creating a Life of Impact

Creating a life of impact means that everything you do—from your personal goals to your relationships to your career—reflects your desire to make a positive difference. It involves aligning your daily actions with a broader mission, so that each step you take brings you closer to leaving the world better than you found it.

One way to create impact is by leading by example. Whether you realize it or not, people are watching how you live your life. Your actions, words, and choices inspire others to follow suit. By living with integrity, kindness, and purpose, you become a role model for others, showing them what's possible when you commit to something bigger than yourself.

Another way to create a lasting impact is by dedicating yourself to continuous growth. The more you develop your skills, knowledge, and character, the more you can give to others. Personal growth isn't just about improving your own life; it's about becoming a better resource for those around you.

Lastly, impact comes from persistence. You don't need to make sweeping changes overnight. Small, consistent efforts over time can lead to profound results. Whether it's mentoring someone in your field, helping a friend in need, or volunteering a few hours a week, these small acts of service accumulate into a significant impact over the course of a lifetime.

How to Inspire and Lead Others
Inspiring and leading others doesn't always mean holding a formal leadership

role. Anyone can lead by example and inspire others to pursue their best selves. The key is to live authentically, with purpose, and in a way that reflects the values you wish to pass on.

To inspire others, start by sharing your story. Whether you've overcome challenges, built a successful career, or found a meaningful way to contribute to society, your journey can serve as a source of inspiration for others. When people see what's possible through your actions, they are more likely to believe in their own potential.

Leadership is also about empowering others. This can involve mentoring someone who's just starting out, supporting a friend or colleague, or even simply listening and offering advice. Empowerment isn't about telling people what to do; it's about helping them see their own strengths and guiding them toward their goals.

Moreover, a true leader fosters collaboration. They understand that they don't have to do everything alone and that working together with others can create a much larger impact. By building teams and fostering partnerships, you can multiply your efforts and bring out the best in everyone around you.

Living a Legacy That Outlives You
Leaving a legacy that outlives you is perhaps the ultimate measure of a life well-lived. It's about ensuring that your impact continues long after you're gone. This doesn't necessarily mean leaving behind a monument or your name in history books—it's about the values, ideas, and contributions you pass on to others.

One of the most powerful ways to live a legacy that outlives you is through the people you influence. Whether it's your family, friends, colleagues, or even people you've never met, the values you teach and the support you offer can be passed on through generations. The ripple effect of your actions can spread far beyond what you might ever see.

Another way to live a lasting legacy is by creating something tangible that will endure. This could be a business, a charity, a piece of art, or a body of work that reflects your values and continues to make a difference long after you're gone. For example, if you write a book, start a foundation, or build a school, your contributions will continue to touch lives even in your absence.

Living a legacy also means being intentional about your daily actions. Every choice you make is an opportunity to contribute to your legacy. It's not about waiting for the right moment to start making a difference, but about living with purpose every single day.

In the end, a legacy isn't about fame or recognition. It's about knowing that you've made a positive impact on the world and that the life you've lived will continue to inspire, support, and uplift others long after you're gone.

Leaving a lasting legacy is an essential part of living an extraordinary life. By giving back, contributing to causes that align with your values, and creating a life of impact, you can ensure that your legacy continues to touch lives and inspire others. Whether through the people you help or the work you leave behind, your contributions will live on, making the world a better place for future generations.

CONCLUSION

EMBRACING THE JOURNEY, NOT JUST THE DESTINATION

As you work towards living an extraordinary life, it's easy to become fixated on reaching the end goal—whether that's success, happiness, or fulfillment. However, one of the most valuable lessons you can learn is that life isn't just about the destination, but about the journey that takes you there. The experiences, challenges, and growth that occur along the way are just as important, if not more so, than the ultimate outcome.

Embracing the journey means being present and fully engaged in your daily life. Rather than rushing toward the next milestone, take time to appreciate where you are right now. Every day brings new opportunities for learning, connection, and growth. These moments, however small, shape who you become. By focusing on the present, you can avoid the trap of constantly seeking more and never feeling satisfied.

Moreover, when you embrace the journey, you open yourself up to unexpected experiences and possibilities. Life rarely unfolds exactly as planned, and the path to an extraordinary life is often winding and unpredictable. But within those detours and challenges lie the moments that make life rich and rewarding. The twists and turns you encounter will build your resilience, creativity, and strength.

Another key aspect of embracing the journey is recognizing that setbacks and failures are not roadblocks but part of the process. Every stumble is a chance to learn something new and gain perspective. If you see these experiences as stepping stones rather than obstacles, they can become some of the most valuable parts of your journey. Instead of being discouraged by difficulties, you can view them as essential elements of your growth.

By embracing the journey, you'll find that the pressure to constantly achieve or "arrive" at a certain point lessens. You'll begin to see that living an extraordinary life isn't about checking off boxes or hitting specific targets, but about how you navigate the path to those goals. It's about the relationships you build, the values you live by, and the impact you make along the way.

Celebrating Your Progress, No Matter How Small

One of the most overlooked aspects of personal growth is the importance of celebrating your progress. Too often, people are so focused on their ultimate goals that they forget to acknowledge the small victories along the way. However, celebrating your progress—no matter how small—can have a profound impact on your motivation, confidence, and overall sense of fulfillment.

Each step you take, each obstacle you overcome, is a testament to your dedication and effort. Whether it's completing a task, overcoming a personal fear, or simply sticking to a positive habit, these moments deserve recognition. By celebrating these small achievements, you reinforce the idea that you are capable of growth and change, which fuels your determination to keep moving forward.

Celebrating progress also helps to shift your mindset from one of scarcity to one of abundance. Rather than constantly feeling like you haven't done enough, you start to see how far you've come. This shift can reduce feelings of self-doubt and inadequacy, replacing them with a sense of pride and accomplishment.

In addition, taking time to reflect on your progress allows you to gain perspective on your journey. It's easy to lose sight of how much you've achieved when you're focused on the next goal. But by pausing to look back, you can see the progress you've made, the challenges you've overcome, and the growth you've experienced. This reflection can be incredibly empowering and can remind you of your own resilience and capacity for change.

Moreover, celebrating small wins can help you stay motivated and avoid burnout. When the road to an extraordinary life feels long or overwhelming, these celebrations can serve as a source of encouragement. They remind you that progress is being made, even if it's not immediately obvious, and that every step counts.

It's important to note that celebrating progress doesn't always have to be grand or public. Sometimes it's a quiet moment of reflection, journaling about what you've achieved, or simply taking a break to appreciate your hard work. The key is to acknowledge your efforts and give yourself credit for the strides you're making.

Final Words on Living an Extraordinary Life

Living an extraordinary life isn't about perfection, nor is it about wealth, fame, or outward success. It's about living authentically, with purpose, passion, and intention. It's about cultivating the right mindset, building meaningful relationships, overcoming challenges with grace, and leaving a positive impact on the world.

An extraordinary life is deeply personal—it looks different for everyone. For some, it might mean pursuing a career that brings joy and fulfillment. For others, it could be about nurturing strong relationships with family and friends or contributing to causes that matter. The common thread, however, is living in a way that aligns with your values and brings out the best in yourself and others.

There will be times when the journey feels difficult, and you may question whether it's all worth it. You might face setbacks, doubt yourself, or wonder if you're on the right path. In these moments, remember that extraordinary lives are not built in a day. They are crafted through small, consistent actions over time, through the willingness to learn and grow, and through the courage to keep going even when things are tough.

As you continue on your path, give yourself permission to dream big, but also remember to stay grounded in the present. Don't wait for some future moment to start living the life you want. You are already on the journey, and every step you take, no matter how small, is part of your extraordinary story.

In the end, living an extraordinary life is not about reaching a destination—it's about how you live each day. It's about the choices you make, the people you touch, and the legacy you leave behind. And most importantly, it's about finding joy, meaning, and fulfillment in the process of becoming the best version of yourself.

So, as you move forward, embrace the journey, celebrate your progress, and live with the knowledge that you have the power to create an extraordinary life, one that reflects your deepest values, passions, and purpose.

www.ingramcontent.com/pod-product-compliance
Lightning Source LLC
Chambersburg PA
CBHW050305230526
45471CB00005B/2037